ENTERTAINMENT
ROBOTS

BY ASHLEY STREHLE HARTMAN

CONTENT CONSULTANT
Pranav A. Bhounsule
Assistant Professor of Mechanical Engineering
University of Texas at San Antonio

P9-DFR-641

robot dances at an electronics
China.

Core Library

An Imprint of Abdo Publishing
abdopublishing.com

abdopublishing.com

Published by Abdo Publishing, a division of ABDO, PO Box 398166,
Minneapolis, Minnesota 55439. Copyright © 2019 by Abdo Consulting
Group, Inc. International copyrights reserved in all countries. No part of this
book may be reproduced in any form without written permission from the
publisher. Core Library™ is a trademark and logo of Abdo Publishing.

Printed in the United States of America, North Mankato, Minnesota
032018
092018

Cover Photo: Bai Kelin/Imaginechina/AP Images
Interior Photos: Bai Kelin/Imaginechina/AP Images, 1; Yoshio Tsunoda/AFLO/Newscom, 4–5;
iStockphoto, 7, 27 (top left), 45; Red Line Editorial, 9; Sotheby's/akg-images/Newscom, 12–13;
Keystone-France/Gamma-Keystone/Getty Images, 15; AP Images, 16; Tsugufumi Matsumoto/AP
Images, 19; Shutterstock Images, 20–21, 27 (top middle); Marina Grigorivna/Shutterstock Images,
23, 43; Tony Gutierrez/AP Images, 26, 27 (bottom); Wave Break Media/Shutterstock Images, 27
(top right); Jae C. Hong/AP Images, 28–29; Bizu Tesfaye/Sipa USA/Newscom, 31; Zhang Peng/
LightRocket/Getty Images, 33; Peter Menzel/Science Source, 36–37; Kyodo/AP Images, 40

Editor: Bradley Cole
Imprint Designer: Maggie Villaume
Series Design Direction: Ryan Gale

Library of Congress Control Number: 2017962796

Publisher's Cataloging-in-Publication Data

Names: Strehle Hartman, Ashley, author.
Title: Entertainment robots / by Ashley Strehle Hartman.
Description: Minneapolis, Minnesota : Abdo Publishing, 2019. | Series: Robot innovations |
    Includes online resources and index.
Identifiers: ISBN 9781532114663 (lib.bdg.) | ISBN 9781641852746 (pbk) |
    ISBN 9781532154492 (ebook)
Subjects: LCSH: Personal robotics--Juvenile literature. | Electric toys--Juvenile literature. |
    Robotic pets--Juvenile literature. | Robots--Juvenile literature.
Classification: DDC 629.892--dc23

Distributed in paperback by North Star Editions, Inc.

CONTENTS

CHAPTER
ONE

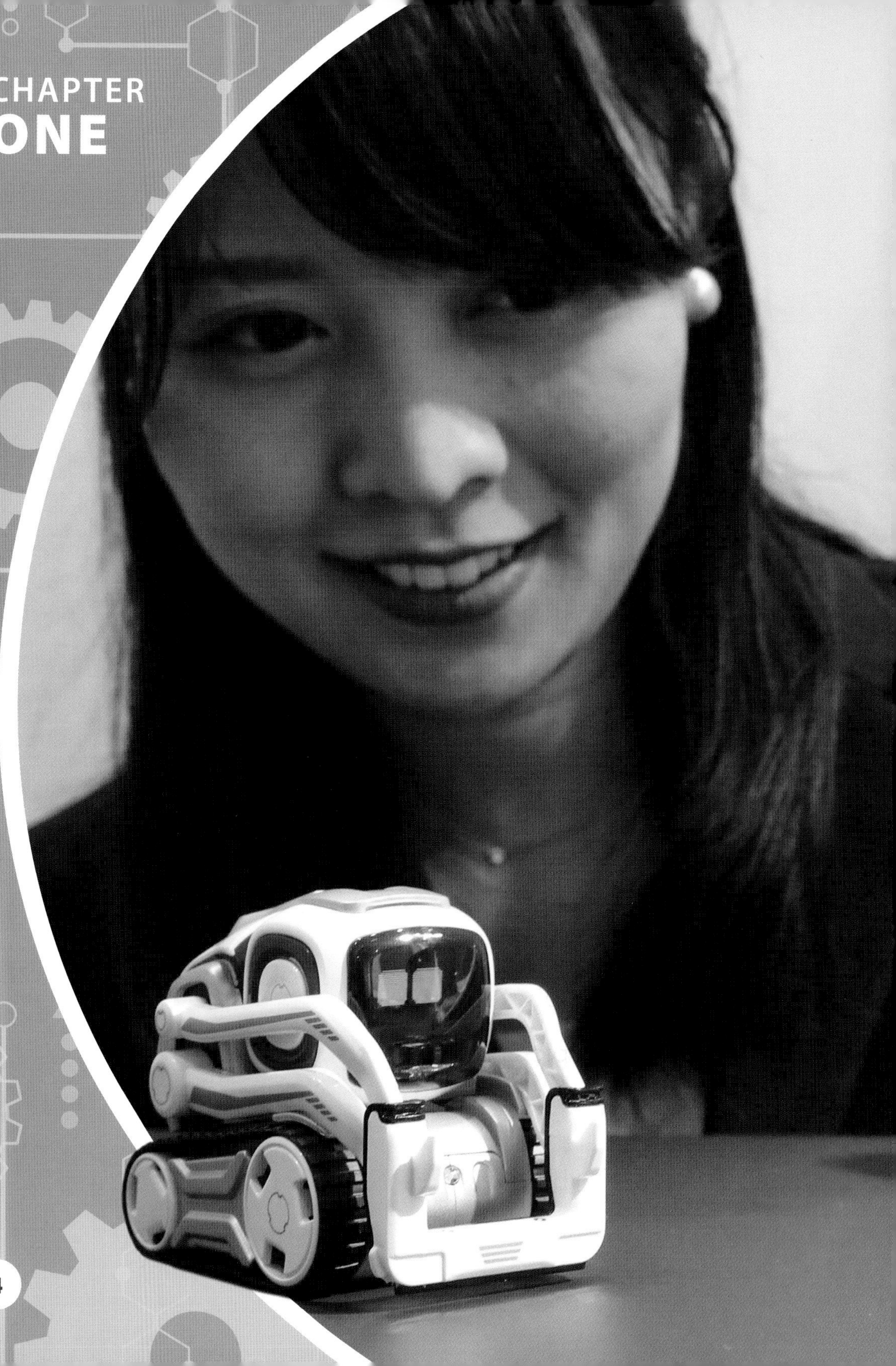

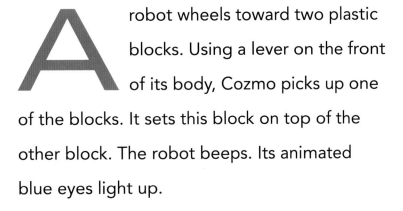

WHAT IS A ROBOT?

A robot wheels toward two plastic blocks. Using a lever on the front of its body, Cozmo picks up one of the blocks. It sets this block on top of the other block. The robot beeps. Its animated blue eyes light up.

A woman brings over a third block. She points to the top of the second block. She wants the third block stacked here. But the robot is too short. It can't reach. The woman picks up the block and stacks it herself.

The robot wheels over to the stacked blocks and knocks them down. It rolls away,

Cozmo is a robot that can learn about its environment.

DESIGNING ROBOTS

ANKI

Anki is a robotics company based in San Francisco, California. It was founded by three graduates of Carnegie Mellon University's Robotics Institute. It is best known for its toy robot, Cozmo. Anki's president and founder is Hanns Tappeiner. He said Cozmo is like "a Pixar robot come to life." There's a good reason for this. Anki hired former employees from Pixar, the animation studio behind movies such as *WALL-E*. They also hired a group of animators to design Cozmo's movement and behavior. Anki tries to make robots that don't seem like robots. "Not playing with Cozmo for a week should feel like not playing with your puppy for a week," said Boris Sofman, another Anki founder.

making a noise designed to sound like laughter.

DIFFERENT KINDS OF ROBOTS

When most people think of robots, they think of robots that are made to work. Some of these robots work in factories. Some of them go places that are dangerous for people to go, such as space. But some robots are made just for fun. Cozmo, the block-stacking robot,

A robotic arm works in a factory.

is this kind of robot. He is an entertainment robot made to play with people.

Robot scientists, called roboticists, make robots for lots of different reasons and to do many different jobs. That means robots can look very different. Some are playful robots such as Cozmo. Others are mechanical-arm robots used in factories. Some robots assemble or paint cars. There are many kinds of robots.

WHAT ALL ROBOTS DO

Most robots have three things in common. First, robots often have sensors. These are like the eyes and ears of the robot. Second, robots have computer processors. These act like the robot's brain. They allow it to follow instructions or even make decisions on its own. Third, robots have actuators. Actuators are motors that allow the robot to react to its environment.

For an example of these parts in action, imagine a wheeled robot moving around a room. With its sensors, the robot notices that it is about to run into a wall. The robot uses its processor to think about this situation. It has been instructed to avoid walls. It uses its actuators, attached to wheels, to turn away from the danger. This pattern of behavior is called "sense-think-act." Robots do each of these steps, but not all machines that do these steps are robots. An air conditioner can sense with a thermostat, think with a computer, and act with its cooling system. But an air conditioner is not a robot.

THE SENSE-THINK-ACT
PATTERN

This diagram shows the sense-think-act-pattern.
This is a pattern that robots can use to respond to their
environment. How does this diagram help explain robot
behavior? Give an example of how a robot would use
this pattern.

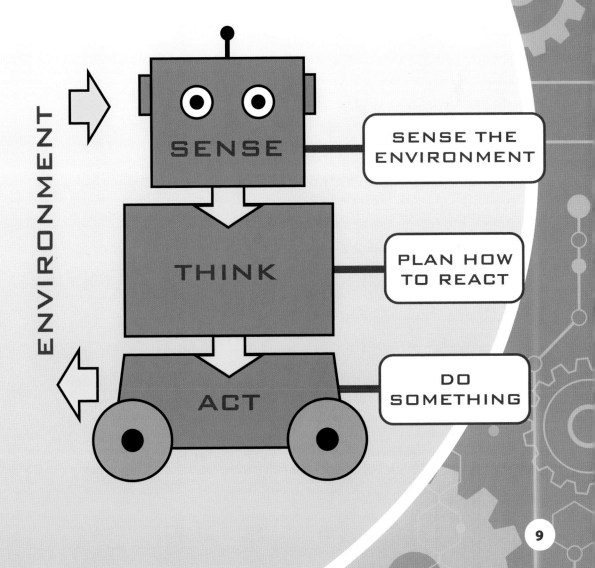

ENTERTAINMENT ROBOTS

Entertainment robots are unique. They're the only robots designed just to amuse people. People have been creating robots like this for a long time. However, today's robots are smarter and cheaper than ever before. As more people can afford these robots, they're becoming a bigger part of everyday life.

THE FIRST USE OF THE WORD *ROBOT*

The word *robot* was first used in 1920. It is from the play "Rossum's Universal Robots" by Karel Čapek. In the play, a factory uses artificial humans as workers. Čapek calls these creations *robots*. These robots are happy to work for people at first. But later, they change their minds and revolt against their human bosses. Čapek chose the word *robot* on purpose. It comes from the Slavic word *robota*, which means "forced labor."

STRAIGHT TO THE
SOURCE

Cozmo, the block-stacking robot, was based on robots from movies. One of Cozmo's creators explains why Anki, the company behind the robot, is inspired by movie characters:

> Cozmo is the result of a quest by Anki president and cofounder, Hanns Tappeiner, to bring movie robots such as *Short Circuit's* Johnny Five, *Star Wars's* R2-D2 or *Wall-E* into the real world. "We watched a lot of movies, and it became obvious that it's very easy to forge an emotional connection with a movie robot. . . . And that was so different from the functional robots we saw on a daily basis at Carnegie Mellon." . . . Tappeiner's team focused hard on creating a robot that was as engaging. "One of the fundamental things we've figured out in the last few years is that character and personality in technology are going to be a really big deal."

> Source: Dan Jolin. "Would You Want a Robot to Be Your Child's Best Friend?" *Guardian*. Guardian, September 10, 2017. Web. Accessed September 20, 2017.

Changing Minds

The text above argues that it is important for robots to have character and personality. Do you agree or disagree with this argument? What reasons and facts would you use to support your opinion?

CHAPTER TWO

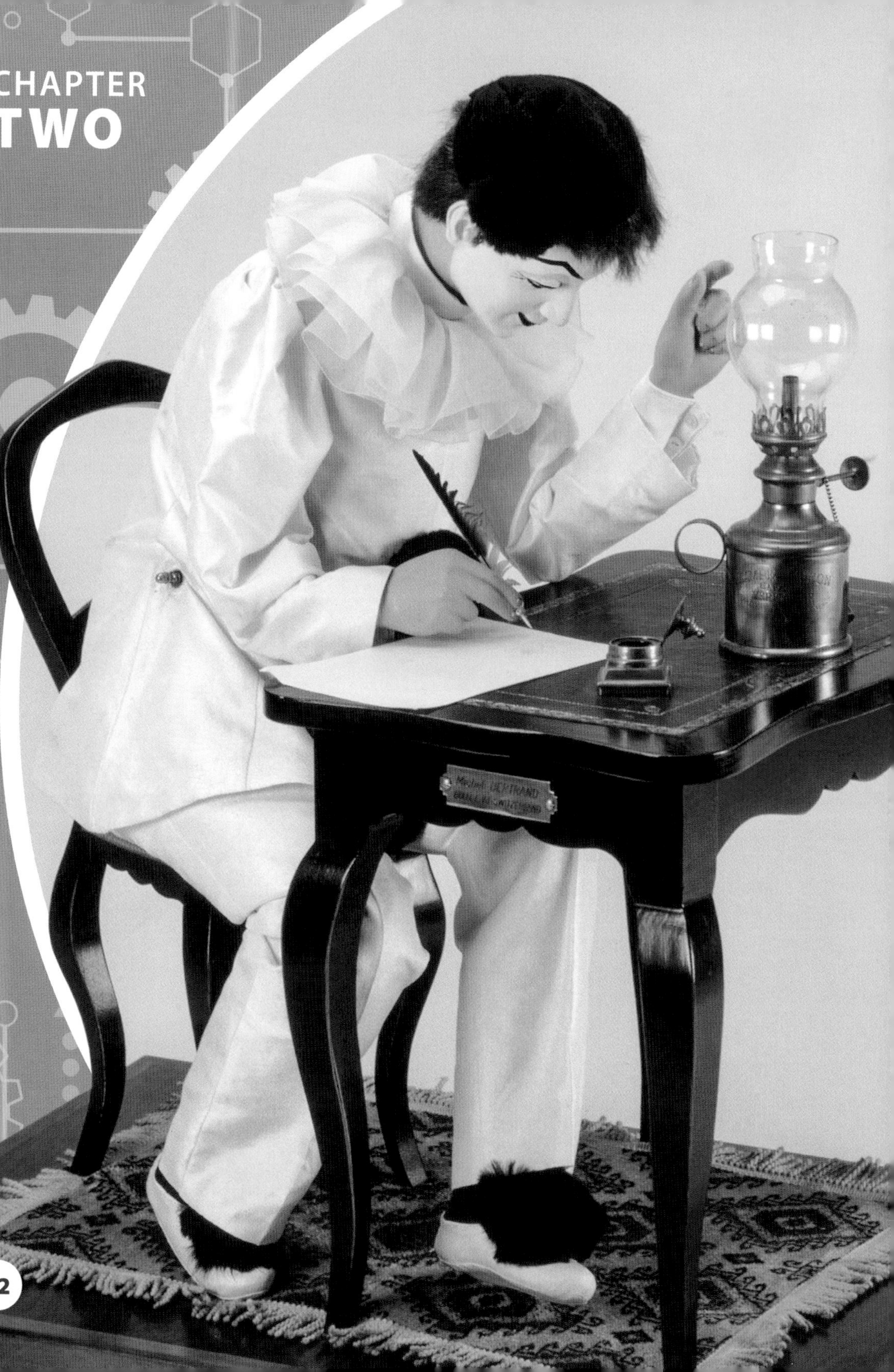

ENTERTAINMENT ROBOTS OF THE PAST

Robots may seem like new creations. But humans have been making robot-like machines for a long time. As early as the 1600s and 1700s, people made mechanical puppets and dolls called automatons to entertain themselves. These machines were complicated, but they could not perform elements of the sense-think-act pattern. They could only act.

In the 1600s in Japan, artists made mechanical puppets called *karakuri ningyō*. This loosely translates as "puppets designed to tease or inspire wonder." These dolls were

This mechanical writer is a complex automaton and an important step in robot history.

controlled by hidden springs and gears. Some of them could even serve people tea.

A century later, Swiss clockmaker Pierre Jaquet-Droz created three mechanical dolls to amuse royalty. One of the dolls wrote, another played music on an organ, and the third doll drew pictures.

The mechanical dolls were controlled by gears, pegs, and springs.

In 1739, Jacques de Vaucanson made a realistic-looking mechanical duck. It could sit, stand, quack, and waddle. The duck also appeared to eat, drink, and go to the bathroom.

JACQUES DE VAUCANSON

Jacques de Vaucanson may be known best for his mechanical duck. But he also played a big part in the development of modern technology. In the mid-1700s, de Vaucanson was the director of the French government's silk mills. In this job, he invented the first patented automatic loom. It used a system of punched cards to program the loom to create patterns in silk. This punch card system inspired modern computer developers.

A woman holds two automaton dolls that appear to play music.

Large crowds gathered to see the duck. It was even presented in the royal court of King Louis XV of France.

MODERN ENTERTAINMENT ROBOTS

By the 1990s, entertainment robots weren't just for royalty any more. Stores started selling them to average people. Furby and AIBO are two of the most well-known entertainment robots.

Furby was released by Tiger Electronics in 1998. The robotic toy was covered in fur like a stuffed animal. It had big plastic eyes, pointy ears, and a small beak. It ran on batteries instead of springs. Furby reacted to sounds and movement. It also talked in its own language called Furbish. Each Furby would slowly start using English to mimic children learning English. Forty million Furbies were sold in the toy's first three years. There have been new editions of Furby ever since.

The robotic dog AIBO was introduced

DESIGNING ROBOTS

SONY'S AIBO

Sony first introduced the AIBO in 1999. It was originally sold in Japan and was later sold in the United States and Europe. Its name comes from Artificial Intelligence roBOt. The first model was the ERS-110. Later models had new features such as LED eyes and more sensors. This allowed AIBO to better interact with its environment.

Tiger Electronics's Furby was a popular holiday item for children in 1999.

by Sony in 1999. It was quite costly at almost $2,000. The original AIBO could walk, bark, and perform tricks. Sony offered updated versions of AIBO until 2006. A new AIBO was announced in 2017. This updated AIBO can learn and download updates from the internet.

The mechanical devices of the 1600s led to the simple entertainment robots of the 1990s. Today, technology has advanced even further. Engineers and designers are creating robots that are smarter and more capable than ever before.

EXPLORE ONLINE

Chapter Two talks about historical robots from all over the world. The article at the website below gives you some more information about AIBO. How does the information on this website compare to what you learned in Chapter Two? What new information did you learn from the website?

SONY AIBO
abdocorelibrary.com/entertainment-robots

A Sony vice president presents AIBO in 2000.

CHAPTER
THREE

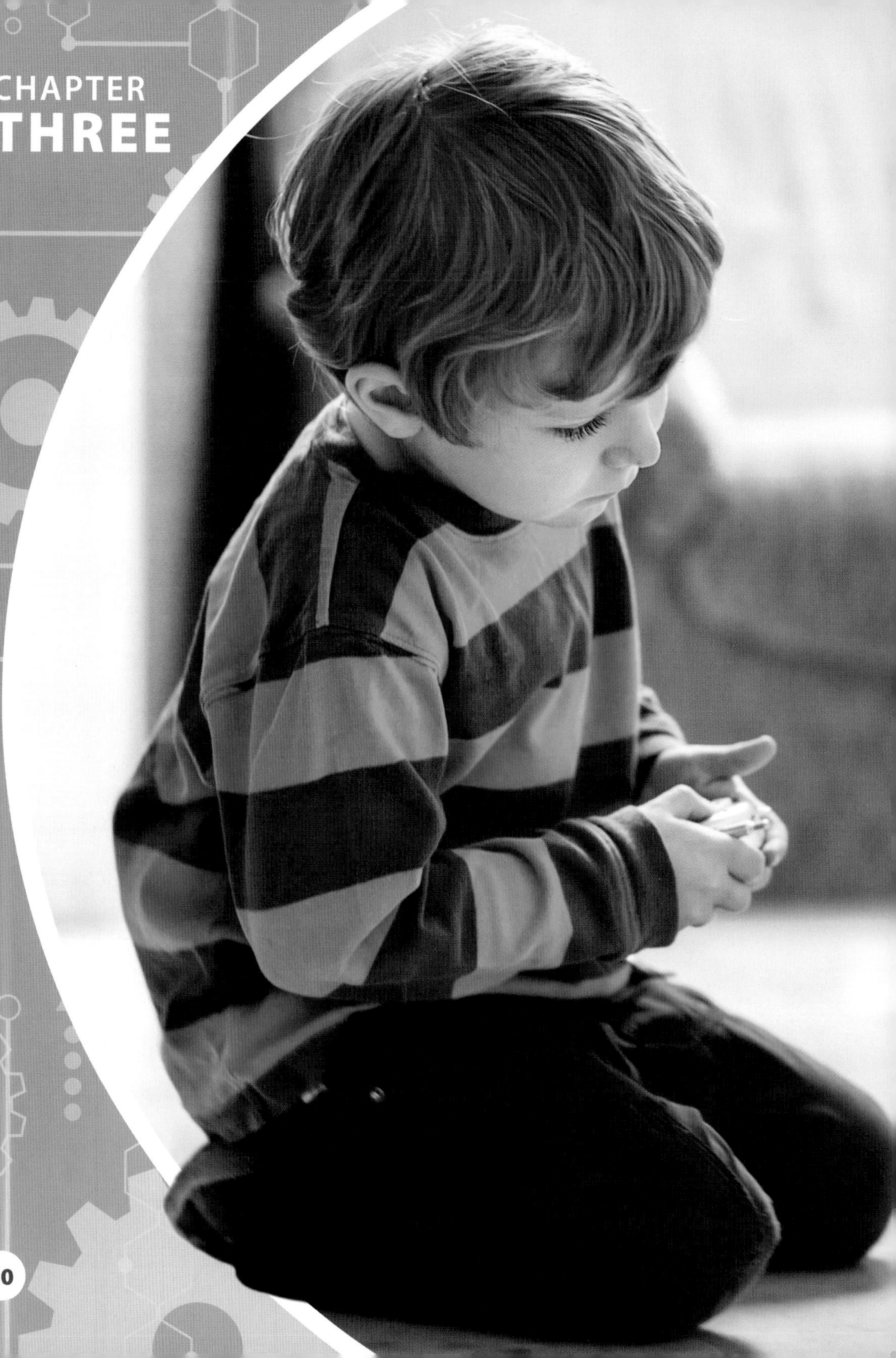

CHALLENGES AND SOLUTIONS

The companies that make entertainment robots have unique challenges. Unlike other robots, entertainment robots are made for people rather than companies. That means these robots have to be affordable. They also have to be something that most people want to buy. Robotics companies use creativity and technology to deal with these challenges.

Some robots are made as toys for children.

KEEPING PRICES LOW

Companies who make industrial or military robots sell their robots to companies or governments. These groups have large budgets to pay for robots. But entertainment robot companies sell their robots to individual people.

Some robotics companies keep their prices low by using 3-D printing. When designing a new robot, companies can use a 3-D printer to make new parts. Before, they might have had to buy these parts from another company. Making these parts

HOW 3-D PRINTING WORKS

New techniques in 3-D printing have helped robotics companies design new robots. One way is using a fused deposition modeling printer. The printer makes shapes by stacking thin layers of heated plastic. These layers build up the shape of the 3-D model. Companies can use 3-D printing when designing new parts for robots.

3-D printers layer thin pieces of material to build 3-D objects.

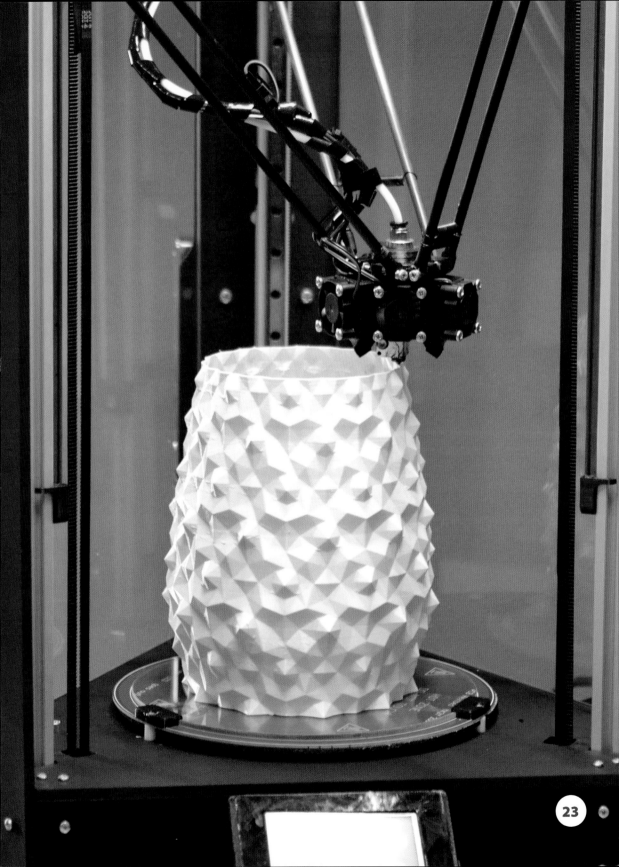

themselves saves the company money. It also saves the company time, because they don't have to wait for the parts. Once the part is made with the 3-D printer, the company makes more with molds. The company can make the parts in bulk, which also saves the company money.

UNCANNY VALLEY

Design is a major challenge for entertainment robot companies. It doesn't matter how cheap a robot is if people don't want to buy it. No one cares what an industrial robot looks like. They just care that it can do its job. But people have to like the way entertainment robots look. People have to want to spend time with their robots. Finding out what people like can be hard.

There is a concept called the "uncanny valley" that explains some negative reactions toward robots. The idea was explained by Japanese roboticist Masahiro Mori in 1970. According to the theory, people like a robot more if it looks like a human. But there's a point where a robot looks almost like a human, but not close enough to be fully realistic. This point is called the "uncanny valley." Robots that look like this may frighten people.

MAKING ROBOTS PEOPLE LIKE

Roboticists approach the "uncanny valley" in two opposite ways. Some make their robots look not human at all. Cozmo, the block-stacking robot, is an example of this kind of robot. Other roboticists try even harder to make their robots look human. That pushes

DESIGNING ROBOTS

DAVID HANSON

David Hanson founded Hanson Robotics. He also worked for Disney's Imagineering Lab. He is known for creating realistic-looking robots. Hanson invented a lifelike skin for his robots called Frubber. Hanson has created more than 20 human-looking robots, including Professor Einstein and Sophia. Professor Einstein is a robotic toy and the first product Hanson Robotics sold to the public. Sophia learns from talking with people. She was interviewed on the show *60 Minutes*.

David Hanson shows off one of his realistic-looking robots.

these robots past the uncanny valley. These robots look so human that people can relate to them comfortably again.

Today, there are popular entertainment robots that look human, and there are robots that look nothing like humans. All of them are designed to be likeable.

THE UNCANNY
VALLEY

This diagram shows the uncanny valley theory.
How does this diagram help you understand this theory?
Think of another type of robot. Decide where it would fit
on this diagram.

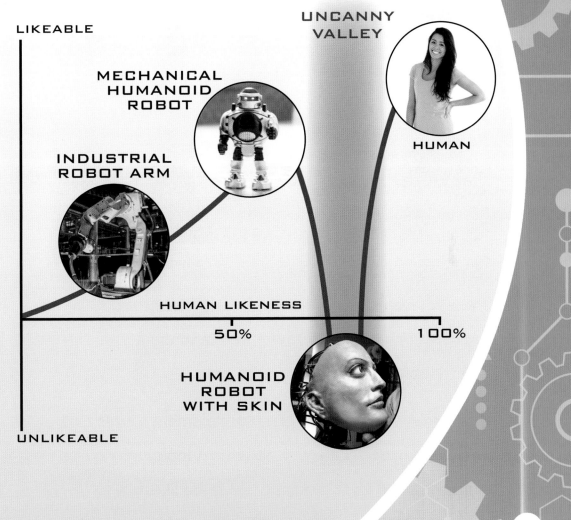

LIKEABLE

UNCANNY
VALLEY

MECHANICAL
HUMANOID
ROBOT

INDUSTRIAL
ROBOT ARM

HUMAN

HUMAN LIKENESS

50%

100%

HUMANOID
ROBOT
WITH SKIN

UNLIKEABLE

CHAPTER FOUR

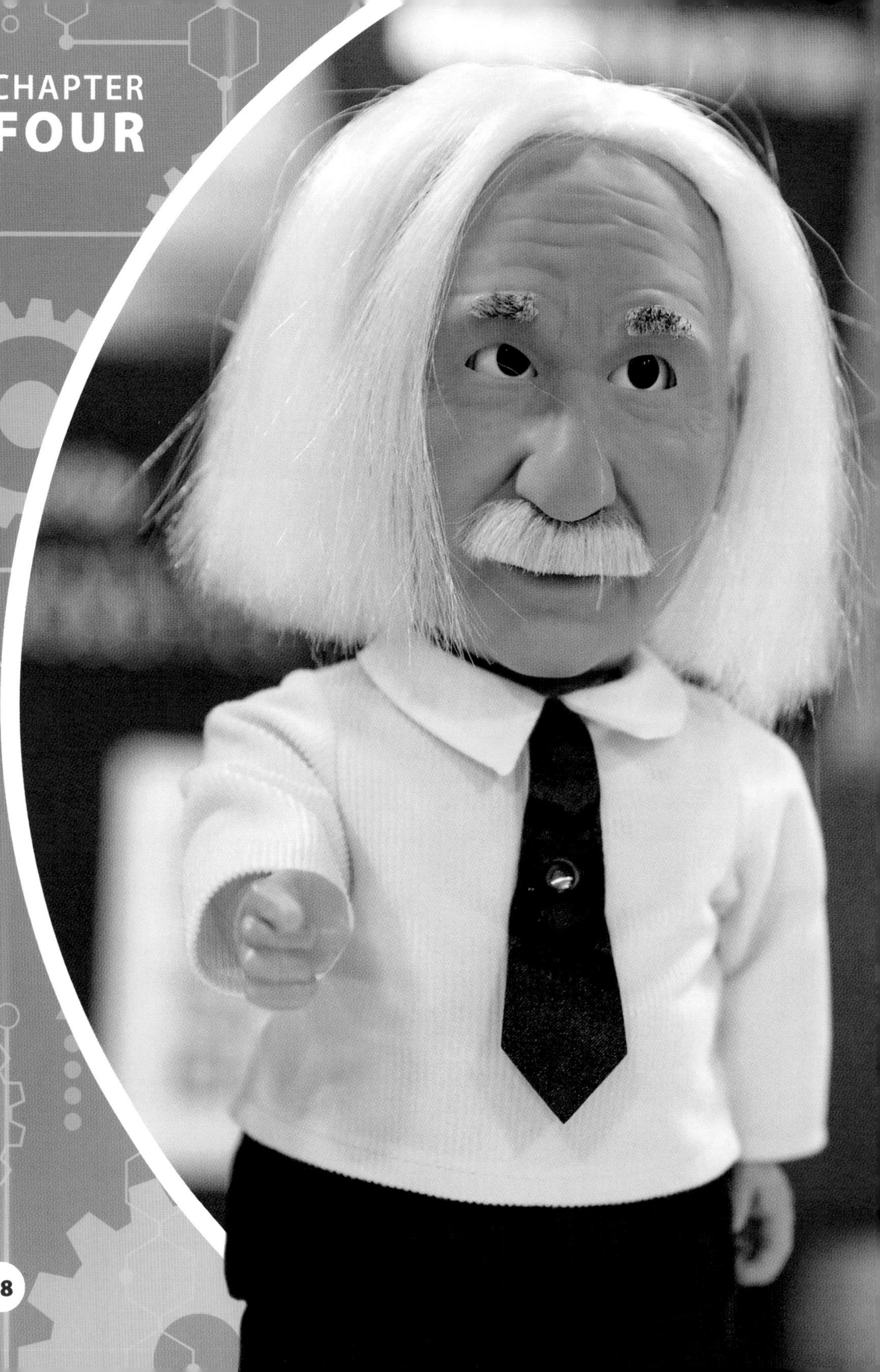

ENTERTAINMENT ROBOTS TODAY

Today's entertainment robots can do more than the robots of the past. They look different than the robots of the past too. Some of them are inspired by famous scientists. Others simply look like balls. But they are all made to entertain.

PROFESSOR EINSTEIN

One robot is called Professor Einstein. It has white hair and a mustache. It looks like a cartoonish version of the physicist Albert Einstein. It is approximately one foot (0.3 m) tall and sits on a tabletop.

Professor Einstein responds to voice commands. It can talk and even tell jokes.

Professor Einstein from Hanson Robotics is displayed at a convention.

Professor Einstein can make more than 50 facial expressions, including sticking out its tongue.

It was designed to be a learning tool for children ages 13 and older. Professor Einstein can help children with homework. It can even teach them about science using interactive apps and games. It can also answer questions like a virtual assistant.

SPHERO

Unlike Professor Einstein, Sphero does not look human.

THE TURING TEST

Robots are designed to interact well with people and appear intelligent. As early as the 1950s, a British scientist designed a test to measure the intelligence of machines. The scientist, Alan Turing, was one of the pioneers of artificial intelligence. His test is called the Turing Test, or the Imitation Game. In this test, a machine and person type back and forth. The person cannot see who is typing messages to them. If the person can't tell whether he or she is talking to a person or a machine, the machine has passed the Turing Test.

Spheros are also made to look like characters from movies such as BB-8 from *Star Wars: The Force Awakens*.

This robotic ball is made by a company of the same name. The robot is made out of white plastic and is approximately the size of an orange. Spheros have small, blue faces printed on them.

Users can link a Sphero to a smartphone or tablet. This way, users can control the ball's movement.

Sphero can travel at up to 5 miles per hour (8 km/h). It also knows the user's location, so users can command the balls to roll back to them. Spheros vibrate and flash lights. They can also flip, navigate obstacles, and dance.

DESIGNING ROBOTS

SPHERO

The robotics company Sphero is based in Colorado. It is best known for its robotic toy Sphero. The toy's inventors and the company's founders are Ian Bernstein and Adam Wilson. They had made other products together, but no one bought them, so they needed a new idea. Bernstein suggested they make "something simple, something I could keep in my pocket, pull it out, throw it on the table, and it does something cool." Wilson suggested a marble. That led to the robotic ball Sphero. The company now sells several versions.

TEGA

Tega is made by the Personal Robots Group at the Massachusetts Institute of Technology (MIT). It has red fur on its body and

Educational robots can help students learn a variety of topics.

blue hair on its head. It has a blue face with big eyes. It was designed to work with preschool children. It helps them improve their language skills and vocabularies through storytelling games.

Tega uses a smartphone to recognize movement and facial expressions. This lets Tega respond to children's behavior. Tega often copies the way children act. For example, Tega acts excited when the child is excited. Tega can also learn what a child likes or doesn't like. This lets Tega create special teaching programs for each child based on his or her preferences. The more children play with their Tegas, the more the robots can personalize their behavior just for them.

Entertainment robots have come a long way. Professor Einstein, Sphero, and Tega are far more advanced than the early robots and mechanical dolls. Roboticists think the robots of the future will be even more impressive.

STRAIGHT TO THE
SOURCE

The passage below is from an interview with Sphero founder Ian Bernstein. In it, he talks about what makes his company unique:

> *In the past companies have viewed robots as either purely utilitarian or primarily toy. We view ourselves as both an entertainment company and a robotics company. This allows us to create connected play experiences like you see in our products to date, but also create extremely sophisticated robotic experiences that are currently in our lab. As adults, kids, and families as a whole become more connected, our products are becoming more and more relevant. Our mission at Sphero is to put a robot in every home, and we don't see any reason we can't make that happen.*

> Source: Jake Slagel. "Our Exclusive Interview with Sphero Founder Ian Bernstein." *The News for The Young Businessmen.* The Young Businesmen, November 9, 2015. Web. Accessed September 20, 2017.

What's the Big Idea?

Take a close look at the passage above. What is the main point the author is trying to make? How does the author support his claim? What connection is the author making between entertainment and robots?

CHAPTER
FIVE

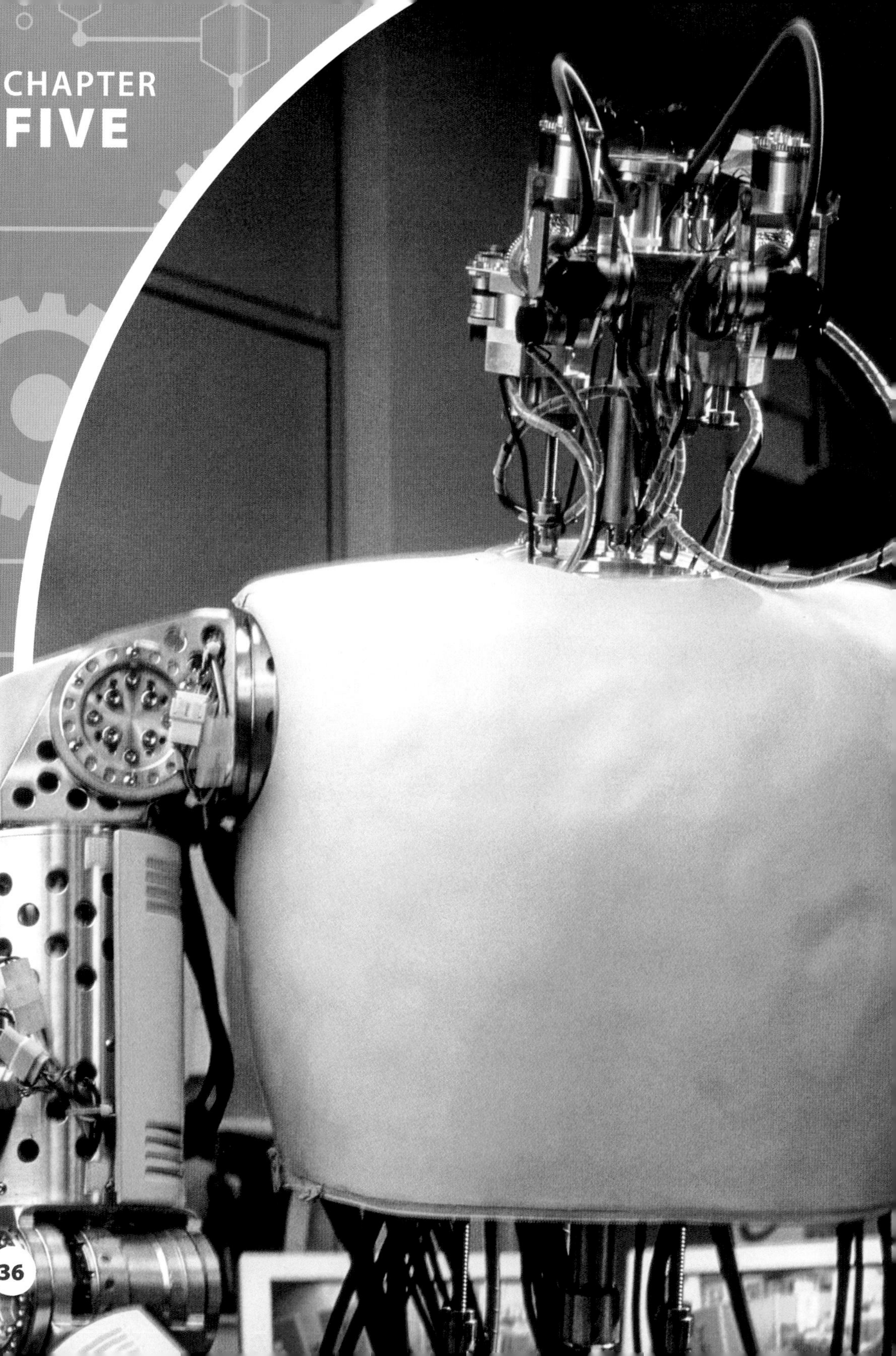

THE FUTURE OF ROBOTS

Robots are now in factories, hospitals, and homes. In the future, roboticists predict that robots will be a more important part of people's lives. These robots will look and act differently than today's robots.

SOFT ROBOTS

Entertainment robots have always been designed to work well with people. But roboticists think there are more ways to improve robots that interact with people. Being soft or flexible could help robots be even better.

A robot is covered in padding to help it interact with people more safely.

SOFT ROBOTS INSPIRED BY NATURE

Roboticists turned to nature to find better ways for robots to move. That's why many new soft robots are based on animals. One of the first soft robots was based on an octopus. A scientist brought a live octopus to her lab so she could study it with her students. They built a robot with artificial tentacles that could copy the animal's movements. Roboticists have also made robots based on caterpillars, fish, and jellyfish.

In recent years, scientists have started making robots with soft, flexible materials. Hard, metal robots have limited movement. Soft robots are able to bend, twist, and stretch. In the future, these movements will let robots interact with people in different ways.

Disney has already started making soft robots. In spring 2017, it applied for a patent to make humanoid robots. These robots are made to interact with children and are supposed to be soft and durable. Soft robots could touch and hug people without hurting or pinching them. Disney 3-D printed the robot's joints. The robot was then covered in a soft material. Disney hasn't introduced these robots to the public yet. However, it currently uses robots with sound recordings in its theme parks.

LEARNING ROBOTS

Sophia, a robot made for talking, can use artificial intelligence to study dialogue. This helps it improve its future conversations. It learns from observing and from engaging.

Pepper can read people's emotions by sensing their tone of voice. It can

DESIGNING ROBOTS

CYNTHIA BREAZEAL

Cynthia Breazeal is a professor at the Massachusetts Institute of Technology. She builds robots that interact with people, such as Jibo. She saw the 1977 movie *Star Wars* and loved the movie's robots R2-D2 and C-3PO. Later, she watched robotic rovers land on Mars. She thought it was strange that people could send robots into space, but they didn't have them in their homes.

Pepper entertains a group of children.

also detect nonverbal behavior, like facial expressions. Pepper was the first humanoid robot introduced to homes in Japan. Roboticists expect robots to get even better at these skills. This will make robots more useful and accepted.

MULTITASKING ROBOT COMPANIONS

Now many robots are designed for one task. For example, the Roomba robot is designed just to vacuum. In the future, roboticists think robots will become multitaskers. These robots will entertain and interact with people more like a human would. They will be able to handle more duties rather than being designed for a single task.

These new skills will make robots more popular. These robots will have unique personalities and be able to talk with people like a member of the family. The entertainment robots of the future will be very different from mechanical dolls and Furbies, but they will still entertain.

ROBOT COMPANIONS

Chapter Five talked about what robots may be like in the future. It discussed how they will look and behave, as well as how people will interact with them. What was the main point of this chapter? Read the article at the website below. Does the information in this article relate to what you read in Chapter Five? Does it support what you read or add new information?

WIRED: "COMPANION ROBOTS ARE HERE. JUST DON'T FALL IN LOVE WITH THEM"
abdocorelibrary.com/entertainment-robots

FAST FACTS

- Roboticists make robots for lots of different reasons and to do many different jobs.

- A machine has three main parts to be a robot: sensors, processors, and actuators.

- Robots respond to their environment using a "sense-think-act" pattern of behavior.

- Entertainment robots are unique because they're the only robots designed just to amuse people.

- The word *robot* was first used in the play *Rossum's Universal Robots* in 1920.

- In the 1600s, Japanese artists made mechanical puppets that could serve people tea.

- In the 1700s, a Swiss clockmaker made mechanical dolls that could write, play music on an organ, and draw pictures.

- The Furby and the robotic dog AIBO were two of the most popular robots of the 1990s.

- Entertainment robot companies have to make their robots cheap enough for the average person to afford them.

- Some robot companies use 3-D printing to help make their robots.

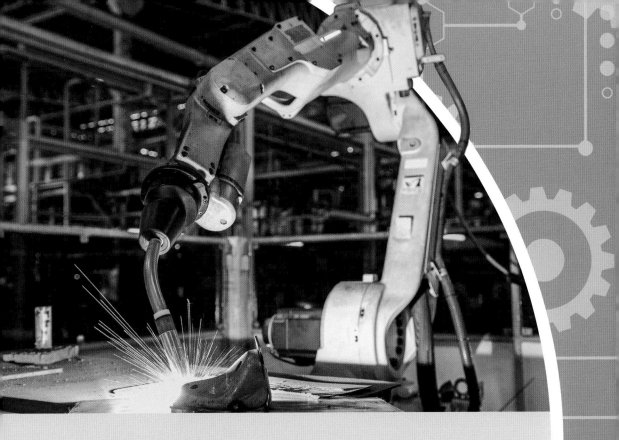

- The concept of the uncanny valley describes people's reactions to robots who look somewhat like humans but are not similar enough to be convincing.

- In the future, there may be more robots made of softer, more flexible materials.

- Some soft robots are based on animals like octopuses, fish, jellyfish, and caterpillars.

- Some robots can already learn from past experiences to improve their interactions with people.

- In the future, roboticists think robots will be better at interacting with people and multitasking.

STOP AND
THINK

Tell the Tale

Chapter One of this book talks about how a robot uses the "sense-think-act" pattern to react to its environment. Imagine you are watching a robot in action. Write a few paragraphs about how the robot uses this pattern to perform tasks.

Dig Deeper

After reading this book, what questions do you still have about entertainment robots? With the help of an adult, find a few trustworthy sources to help answer your questions. Write a paragraph about what you learned.

Another View

This book talks about what robots may be like in the future. But every source is different. Ask an adult to help you find another source that talks about the future of robots. Write a short essay comparing what you learned from that book to what you learned from this book. How are the sources similar? How are they different?

Take a Stand

Some roboticists think that robots should be programmed to have feelings and emotions. Do you think that this is a good idea? Why or why not? Write a paragraph explaining your opinion and your reasons for that opinion.

GLOSSARY

actuator
a motor part of a robot that helps it interact with its environment

artificial intelligence
the ability of a computer to think and make decisions on its own

humanoid robot
a robot made to look like a person

industrial robot
a robot used in factories

mechanical
machine-like

patent
a document that gives a person or company the ownership of a certain invention or product

physicist
a scientist who studies matter and energy

sensor
the part of a robot that lets it see its environment

3-D printing
a technology that lets people create objects using a specially designed printer

ONLINE
RESOURCES

To learn more about entertainment robots, visit our free resource websites below.

Visit **abdocorelibrary.com** for free Common Core resources for teachers and students, including vetted activities, multimedia, and booklinks, for deeper subject comprehension.

Visit **abdobooklinks.com** for free additional online weblinks for further learning. These links are routinely monitored and updated to provide the most current information available.

LEARN
MORE

Koontz, Robin. *Robotics in the Real World.* Minneapolis, MN: Abdo Publishing, 2015.

Mason, Adrienne. *ROBOTS.* Boston, MA: Kids Can Press, 2008.

INDEX

About the Author

Ashley Strehle Hartman is a journalist and writer. She lives in Nebraska with her husband and their dog. When she's not learning about robots, she writes an entertainment column for a local newspaper and blogs about baking.